Screamer on Line Two

by

Phil Hart

Grosvenor House
Publishing Limited

This book is published by
Grosvenor House Publishing Ltd
28-30 High Street, Guildford, Surrey, GU1 3HY.
www.grosvenorhousepublishing.co.uk

A CIP record for this book
is available from the British Library

ISBN 978-1-907211-85-0

Winston Churchill was quoted as saying...

'You can measure the civilisation of a country by the way it treats its prisoners'

I have often thought that this can be paraphrased to...

'You can measure the service of a company by the way it deals with its complaints'

Dedication

I would like to dedicate this book to all the companies that my friends, family and colleagues have had reason to complain to in the past 30 years, who have treated the complaints poorly. Without these companies, there would have been no need for this book!

Contents

CHAPTER ONE
INTRODUCTION

'The post has just arrived love,' shouted Derek to his wife, Dot, from halfway up the stairs. He was going up to get ready to pop out to get his paper and meet Bill and Tony for a morning cuppa.

'OK, thanks darling,' said Dot as she got up and went to pick up the mail from the mat.

'Typical!' she said. **'Bloody typical!'** as she glanced at the mail.

Derek was at the top of the stairs as he thought, **'Here we go again.'**

'That insurance company has got my, no, *our* name wrong again. I was very clear when I said Clarke had an "e" in it. I even told them where the "e" was supposed to go!'

'Does it really matter, darling?' said Derek, sensing an issue building.

'Yes, it does. If they can't get my name right, then what else is wrong?'

Derek started to feel uneasy and did not want to get involved. He knew how precise she could be. His thoughts were focussed on slipping out of the door as smoothly as possible.

Dot opened the letter and began reading the contents. It was a new policy she had taken with APPLEX Insurance and she wanted to ensure it was all in order.

Derek was now back downstairs and quietly, very quietly, slipping on his shoes.

'Oh no!' shouted Dot.

'Oh no!' thought Derek.

'They have left off the cover for the garden. I specifically asked for that.'

A silence ensued when Derek contemplated escaping out the door or responding with a patronising reply.

'AND THEY HAVE CHARGED ME FOR IT!' shouted Dot.

Derek was standing in the hall lacing his second shoe. Now he was in a real quandary; run out the door and risk the wrath of Dot on his return, or go to her in the lounge and join her in the problem. Being of an amiable nature and totally scared of Dot when she was on a mission, he chose the latter.

'I am going to call them to get this sorted out,' said Dot.

'Why not leave it until you need to speak to them for something else? After all, we will be paying for the call. A couple of little errors won't make a big difference,' pleaded Derek.

'Rubbish!' said Dot.

'People should get things right at the start. I won't get angry but will tell them what needs to be corrected. As soon as I have done that you can come with me to the chiropodist.'

Dark clouds gathered over Derek.

'Of course, darling,' he replied, realising now that his cup of tea and chat about last night's game had just gone up in smoke. **'I would love to,'** he said as he slipped off his shoes and put on his slippers again.

Dot put the kettle on and got herself ready for the phone call. She cleared the cat from the armchair and positioned the phone squarely on the coffee table in front of her.

Tea poured, she took up position and, with a straight back and glasses nestled precariously on the end of her nose, she started to dial the number. She was calm and resolute; she was simply going to inform them of the changes required.

As the number was connecting and ringing, she practised what she was going to say under her breath, repeating over and over her first line. The call was answered and Dot readied herself to deliver the well-rehearsed opening.

She did not quite hear the first part of the recorded message as it took a second or two to register that it was not a human voice but, as the recording said, **'...Please choose from one of the following options...'** she focussed on it.

She chose the 'Customer Service' option. It rang again. Again a recorded voice stated,

'All of our agents are busy with other customers at the moment; your call is very important to us, please hold the line and one of our advisors will be with you shortly.'

Dot listened closely to each word of this announcement and, under her breath, muttered how ridiculous it was.

'If I was important they would answer me,' she thought. **'If they had more staff, they might not make all these mistakes,'** she said quietly.

The recorded announcement returned...

'They don't seem to care about me. This is costing me a fortune,' she muttered slightly louder this time.

'Pardon, dear?' said Derek, who had now fished out yesterday's newspaper from the recycling bin and was reading quietly in the corner.

'I said, they don't seem to care about getting things right.'

'Yes, dear. I mean, no, dear,' came the reply from behind the sports pages.

'If they say that I did not tell them the correct spelling, I am going to give them what for,' she muttered.

'And if they say I did not ask for garden cover, I will say to them – how come you are charging me for it then? That will get them.'

Derek knew now not to reply.

'If they say I got it wrong, I will speak to the manager,' she pronounced as the piped music began.

'The Shadows,' she said.

'What?' said Derek.

'They are playing The Shadows down the line to me,' she replied. **'They were never the same without Cliff.'**

No sooner had she finished the sentence than a voice, somewhat louder than the music, came on the line.

'Good morning, APPLEX Insurance, Jane speaking, how can I help?' said Jane in a monotone, machine-like way.

'Good morning,' said Dot. **'My name is Mrs Clarke, with an "e", and I was...'**

'Do you have your postcode?' interrupted Jane.

Somewhat put off her guard and now totally knocked off of her pre-rehearsed opening, Dot could only ask Jane to repeat what she had said.

'Do you have your postcode, please, Mrs Clarke?' repeated Jane.

'DH25 6TD,' Dot sternly responded.

'Now the first line of your address?' enquired Jane.

'Ivy Cottage, Wilderness Lane,' said Dot, again somewhat expectantly. Dot was proud of the quaintness of her address and it often generated interest from people when she offered it. This time, nothing though.

'OK, how can I help you?' said Jane... again!

By this time Dot had collected her thoughts and was back to her rehearsed opening.

'My name is Mrs Clarke with an "e". I purchased a policy from you last week,' she said slowly, clearly and in a very controlled manner, emphasising every word.

'Today I have opened my post only to find you have spelt my name wrong.'

Dot waited for a response or any indication of how Jane was going to receive this news.

'You have come through to the wrong department, you should have gone through to Policy Adjustments. Just transferring you...'

The line went dead.

Jane had gone.

The Shadows returned midway through a song.

'She's gone! She just went! She is transferring me... humph!'

Derek slid lower in the chair, lifting the paper slightly higher. He knew not to respond.

Dot pondered for a moment on what Jane had said and shouted to Derek: **'I had come through to the wrong department, she said... so it's *MY* FAULT... not their phone system... *I* was the one STUPID enough to go through to the wrong department... cheek!**

'Are you listening, Derek? Are you..?'

'Hello, Sales, Paul speaking. How can I help you?' This was a much friendlier greeting and Dot relaxed slightly.

'Yes, I wonder if you can, I was just explaining to Jane that I bought a policy from you last week and you have spelt my name wrong and I need...'

'Can I have your name and postcode, please?' interrupted Paul, his voice somewhat more formal – clearly disappointed that it was not a new sale.

'I gave that to Jane.'

'I need it too,' said Paul.

'Mrs Clarke, with an "e", Ivy Cottage, Wilderness Lane, DH25 6TD.'

'Hold the line, please.'

Dot waited for the music to start but Paul returned quickly this time, **'How do you spell your name then?'**

'C...L...A...R...K...E,' responded Dot.

'OK, that's done now.'

Dot waited momentarily for an apology but to no avail. She continued, **'You have also left off the cover for the garden, but you were quick enough to charge me for it.'**

She was now getting a bit angry; Paul did not seem to care about the error and certainly showed no sign of apologising.

'It does not say "Garden Cover Included" on my screen,' said Paul.

'THEN WHY CHARGE ME FOR IT?' exclaimed Dot.

She now felt as if her honesty is being questioned.

'Anyway, that is not Sales fault, it's Admin; they are always doing things like that. I will have to put you through to Customer Service for that change, as it is on the policy itself.'

The Shadows again!

Dot was fuming at being pushed around with no acknowledgment of how she was feeling, and no responsibility for the error was being taken. She was also fed up of The Shadows!

'Hello, Customer Service, Jane speaking.'

'Jane, it's Mrs Clarke again.'

'Can I have your postcode please?' asked Jane coldly.

'Mrs Clarke, with an "e", Ivy Cottage, Wilderness Lane, DH25 6TD,' said Dot impatiently. She was now standing up and gripping the phone tightly.

Derek remained quiet.

Dot explained the omission. Jane responded that she did not have the authority to alter the policy and she would put it in the work pile for a more senior member of staff to attend to.

Dot now had to actively resist becoming aggressive. All she wanted to do was get some errors corrected. She was feeling as if she had to do the work herself!

'Jane, I am going away next week and need my policy before I go. Can you please ensure this is done?' said Dot in as calm a manner as she could muster.

'By law we have 28 days to issue adjustments,' retorted Jane in a very authoritative way. It seems that she was proud to have the knowledge and the backing of the law.

'This is intolerable,' Dot said, in fact, Dot shouted. **'Who is your Supervisor?'**

'That will be Carol.'

'Carol who?' said Dot, who now seemed to be on a war footing.

'We don't have to give second names,' said Jane, who was relying on rules more and more now.

'Can you put me through to *CAROL* then, please?'

'Sorry, but the Supervisors don't speak to customers. You will have to write in,' said Jane smugly.

This made Dot furious. She resorted to shouting.

'I want the name and address of your Managing Director now, please,' said Dot, being careful not to say something that *she* would not be proud of.

Jane was clearly reading the address for complaints from a card. She said nothing more than the name and address to Dot.

'Thanks for nothing! I will be writing in immediately and also claiming compensation for the calls, postage and my time!' Dot slammed the phone down in temper.

Jane disconnected the call, turned to her colleague saying, **'Blimey, some people... Good morning, APPLEX Insurance'.**

This example shows a somewhat extreme situation of how a simple observation can turn into a Managing Director's letter; or is it an extreme example?

Customers, believe it or not, are very tolerant. They understand that mistakes happen, they make them as well! Although sometimes, the way they behave during some complaints, you could be forgiven for thinking otherwise.

Complaints generally start as observations that something is not right, or something is perceived not to be right. It is the role of the complaint handler to keep it at the level of observation and try to avoid it escalating to a full-blown complaint or even a subsequent demand for compensation. There is more on this subject in the **COMPENSATION** chapter.

It is amazing what power a simple understanding of the mechanics of a complaint can give, combined with some basic skills. If we understand what process most people will travel through, we can usually manage any escalation.

One of the best ways to gauge what is going well and what is not going well in a business is to *speak to the customers*. Many companies spend thousands of pounds on customer research, not realising that there are many phoning in giving you vital information on a daily basis – **FOR FREE!**

There can even be situations where a complaint, handled well, can enhance the relationship with the customer so that it is stronger than the relationships with those who have not complained.

We have all heard statements such as, **'I always use them because if anything goes wrong they sort it out straight away.'** It is not dissimilar to holding a policy with an insurance company; you never know the quality of the company until you make a claim. If the claim goes well, the perceived value of the policy and customer loyalty increases.

Let me explain further. An Insurance Company in the South of England formed a complaint handling team. *All* complaints were logged to the client profiles. After a period of time the company decided to explore how many of those customers stayed with the company following their next policy renewal date. The retention rate was found to be 92%. This in itself does not stand out, until you compare it to the general company retention rate (of those who did not complain) of 87.5%!

This was a clear message that if someone complains and the complaint is dealt with efficiently, then the relationship is enhanced. That company subsequently put an option on the phone system saying, **'If you are dissatisfied with any of our products or services, please press option 5.'** A bold move, but totally logical.

The following chapters will explore:

- What is a complaint?
- The type of complainants
- Understanding customer behaviours
- Compliance and regulations
- Call skills and resolutions
- Suggested statements
- Paying or saving compensation
- A note for Managers and Leaders
- Overall view
- Dot and Derek revisited

Although this book is primarily focussed on complaints made via the telephone, I will be using examples of face-to-face complaints also. The purpose of this is to demonstrate a variety of behaviours that we can all relate to in everyday life, and then show how they manifest themselves in a phone call.

If you can get it right during a phone call, with all the disadvantages that creates, you will get it right face-to-face.

CHAPTER TWO
WHAT IS A COMPLAINT?

We need to be careful when defining exactly what a complaint is. Definitions, by their very nature, encourage us to categorise things. If something has a tight definition, a subject will either fall into that definition, or it will not.

The danger of defining complaints is that when assessing a customer's observation against the definition, it is natural to look for where it does <u>not</u> fit, and then declare **'Great. It's not a complaint!'**

This will lead to the company losing vital research data, have a false representation of satisfaction levels and inferior customer service.

I have heard of other definitions that frankly make no sense to me, they are the **JUSTIFIED** and **NOT JUSTIFIED** complaints.

I find this totally baffling. Who is the judge of whether a complaint is justified or not? Surely if the complainant's expectations of a product or service have not been met and they make *ANY* observation on the matter, then the complaint is justified?

When researching companies that use this type of approach, I realised that what they really meant was **OUR FAULT** or **NOT OUR FAULT**. Another meaning could be **THE CUSTOMER'S EXPECTATIONS WERE RIGHT** or **THE CUSTOMER'S EXPECTATIONS WERE WRONG.**

This is dangerous ground. Is it not the case that the company which is providing the product or service creates the expectation in the customer in the first place? I will concede that many customers will expect more than they actually purchased and will complain when these expectations are not met, but any company must ask itself how the expectation was created in the first place.

- Was it their marketing style?
- Was it the purchase transaction?
- Was it the brand image?
- Are there errors in the promotional material?

By not treating these observations as complaints, there will be a continuing, hidden dissatisfaction with the product or services delivered by that company.

In summary, just because a customer's expectations are deemed to be unreasonable or technically incorrect, this does not give us permission to demote the observation to an **UNJUSTIFIED** level. **ALL COMPLAINTS ARE JUSTIFIED!**

So what is a complaint? I still have not answered.

When is a customer's call, visit or letter deemed a complaint?

It could be said that a complaint is a complaint when the **customer** says it is. Unsurprisingly there are pitfalls here as well.

IS IT ABOUT THE ATTITUDE OF THE CUSTOMER?

Consider the following:

'Good morning, Class Travel, how can I help you?' said Martin as he took the first call of the day.

'Oh, good morning, you answered quickly, I was not expecting that,' said Mrs Thomas meekly.

'Well, it is early and we are not too busy at the moment. How can I help you?' Martin repeated in a very upbeat manner. This was going to be a good call, he thought. It was a nice comment from the customer to set it up.

'Oh yes, I wonder if you can. I have just returned from a holiday I booked with you in Tenerife and I had a wonderful time,' Mrs Thomas explained very slowly and quietly.

'I think I would like to book again for later in the year.'

Martin was now totally relaxed and feeling good about the call. Often early morning calls were known in this business as 'screamers'.

'Of course, Mrs Thomas, no problem. I am glad you had a good time,' said Martin, eagerly awaiting his first sale of the day. **'Would you like the same hotel as before?'**

'Well, no. I hope you don't mind me saying...' Mrs Thomas said in quiet, cautious, almost nervous tones, **'...but the hotel did not match your description. When I booked I was told that the hotel was 10 minutes walking distance from the beach, but in fact it was about 20 minutes. We had to get a cab each day. It was not too much of a problem as we got to know the cab firm staff and they were very helpful.'**

'Oh, OK,' said Martin. **'Do you want me to book you closer to the beach?'**

'Oh, that would be lovely. I am really looking forward to going again,' confirmed Mrs Thomas.

The call continued on to a successful booking and Martin relaxed into his first coffee of the day, proud that he has another satisfied customer (and another few pounds commission for that month).

It is clear that Martin would see no reason why he should register this as a complaint. The call was a re-booking from a seemingly satisfied customer. Consider then if this call was made by someone with a different communication style. The call could be totally different.

'Good morning, Class Travel, how can I help you?' said Martin as he took the first call of the day.

'I want to speak to the Manager,' the customer demanded loudly.

'I am sorry, Madam, but the Manager is in a meeting at the moment. Can I help at all?'

'I doubt it, but my name is Mrs Dunne. I have just come back from a holiday booked through you to Tenerife and the hotel was twice as far away from the beach as you said. This is misrepresentation and I will be contacting the governing bodies to have you investigated!' she shouted. And then, without pausing to take a breath, she carried on.

'I demand compensation and if I do not get it, I will be contacting the television, radio and the papers to get you closed down.' She paused for maximum impact then, in her most menacing voice, proclaimed, **'I am a personal friend of your MD, you know.'**

Now, looking at the two examples, what is the difference in the observation about the position of the hotel? ***Nothing!***

I would assume that Martin would deem the second call a complaint and not the first, when in actual fact there is no difference in the observation. Martin's judgement would be purely based on the attitude of the customer. This would clearly create inconsistencies.

DO WE DECIDE IF THE CUSTOMER IS RIGHT OR WRONG?

Consider the following:

'Good afternoon, Ace Insurance Company, how may I help you?' said David in the busy household claims department.

'Good afternoon, my name is Collins and I would like to make a complaint please,' Mr Collins replied in his most formal voice.

'I am sorry to hear that, can I see if I can assist you?' said David, resigning to a difficult call.

'I hope so, I have had my contents covered with you for many years and now I have just made my first claim - my son's cycle was stolen from the back garden. This morning I received a letter from you stating that it is not covered, as it was not locked. How does that make sense?' Mr Collins paused in anticipation of a positive reply.

'Do you have your policy with you, Mr Collins?'

'Yes, of course I do, I have read it several times today,' said Mr Collins, confident in his efficiency.

'Well, if you look at page 12 under the heading 'Exclusions' and go to number 4, you will see that unlocked cycles are not covered if outside of the home.' David waited.

'Wait there... let me see... hmmmm... I've got it... yes, I can see that now. That's really annoying. I have searched and searched for that. It's really tucked away in very small print. That is typical of you insurance boys. Oh well, guess I will have to leave it.'

'Yes, it is tucked away and we get a lot of calls like this. Not many people read the small print and often find out this way,' said David apologetically.

The call concluded amicably.

In this example, the customer was technically wrong. Does this mean it is not a complaint? It could be said that vital information from the customer was not being logged. Remember that David said that they have to take many calls like this. Does the paperwork need to be modified to stop the calls and provide a better service? How many years has this gone on for and how many more years will it continue?

DO WE JUDGE CUSTOMERS' PERCEPTION?

Often customers' perception of a service or product is totally different to the reality.

PERCEPTION CAN ONLY EXIST WHERE REALITY DOESN'T.

PROVIDE REALITY AND PERCEPTION GOES AWAY

Consider the following:

'Good morning, Greenbelt Camping, John speaking. How can I help you?'

'I wonder if you can,' began a rather annoyed Mr Gordon.

'I sent off for the camping torch you advertised in the Daily People, paid my money and received what can only be described as a tiny pocket torch. I was expecting a full size camping one, which is what I perceived from the picture,' he said, his voice now growing in anger.

'Sorry about that, Mr Gordon. The torches are all the same size and it is a very clear picture.'

'Well, I don't want it now and I have 14 days to send it back so will be doing so immediately,' he retorted.

'Well, I must admit, Mr Gordon, yours is not the first call. If you send it back we will make the refund immediately.'

The transaction was completed.

Would this be recorded as a complaint?
Would it just be recorded as a return of goods and a refund?

The reason for the misunderstanding was possibly a poor picture in the advertisement which encouraged the wrong perception of the size of the torch. Would the company want to carry on using that picture? Would they ever know the extent of the problem if this were not recorded as a complaint?

There is also a school of thought that says complaint handling is just good customer service and does not need to be focussed upon. I agree with the service part of this sentence, but have thoughts on focus. Often in a call, especially a call that starts with a small dissatisfaction, the customer senses they are not getting the acknowledgement they need. As the call progresses, they become more and more angry and then announce:

'Right, this is now a complaint.'

The customer has clearly stepped over an emotional threshold. It is a statement where clearly the customer is expecting a response. To not give a response and to just continue the call as it was, with no acknowledgement, will further annoy the customer. The statement demands acknowledgement and more focussed complaint/resolution handling skills should be evident.

This may simply mean over-emphasising what you were doing anyway, but that in itself is an acknowledgment.

In summary, and in an effort to answer the opening question in this chapter, my definition of a complaint is...

***ANY* CUSTOMER OR POTENTIAL CUSTOMER DISPLAYING *ANY* FORM OF DISSATISFACTION IN *ANY* WAY ABOUT *ANY* PRODUCT, SERVICE OR *ANY* OTHER ASPECTS OF THE BUSINESS.**

CHAPTER THREE
THE COMPLAINANTS

There is a mountain of literature written about the different styles of verbal or written communication. Much of this focuses on psychological theories, based on human responses to information sending and receiving. Many of these are valid, but in my opinion these can be categorised in a few personality types.

Before we look at the descriptions, it must be remembered that there is a simple common theme to all of these people:

They have not had their expectations met

All complainants should be shown the same level of respect. The same duty of care and response should be applied to all. Many of the characteristics shown below will only be evident at the start of a call, or if the call is mishandled. If the complaint handler has done a good job, the extreme behaviours exhibited by angry complainants will be diluted and an efficient communication level will be achieved.

I would say at this stage, despite the descriptions and illustrations in the following pages, no gender is particularly dominant in any category!

The Screamer

The Screamer is loud, demanding and often rude. She does not allow you space to speak. As soon as you think she has stopped, you quickly realise she is merely pausing for breath. She uses the words ***'YOU'*** a lot. He links sentences with statements such as, ***'AND ANOTHER THING…'***

The poor complaint handler will often be in a state of high anxiety. You may see him literally holding the telephone away from his ear, or, more subtly, 'switching off' from the caller. If the complaint is face-to-face, the complaint handler may feel compelled to raise his palms to separate himself from the barrage. This is the person you tell your wife or husband about when you get home. You mutter phrases that include **'dark alleys'** and **'shotguns'.**

The Stealth

This person does not give anything away. He often calls for one reason and then slips the complaint in on the way. He will begin the call with minimal information and wait for the call handler to speak. He will ask lots of questions like, **'What is showing on your screen about the call I made last week?'** He gathers evidence and uses it like a barrister in a court of law. It can take some time for The Stealth to actually utter his complaint but when he does, you can be assured that he will have all the facts and figures to hand.

This is an incredibly frustrating call for the complaint handler, as she is oblivious to the danger until the killer bite. These people are difficult to communicate with and you will struggle to avoid thoughts such as **'slippery'** and **'devious'**.

The Know-All

The Know-All tells you what you have done wrong, what needs to be done, how it needs to be completed, with a structured time frame. He is very precise and demands total accuracy. He will not allow you to prove him wrong on even the smallest point. He will either already be an expert on the subject, or at the very least will have researched thoroughly prior to his call, in order to convince you that he is the expert and you are the idiot.

He will delight in quoting news articles, codes of conduct, regulatory authority rulings and Acts of Parliament. He will, of course, be a 'personal friend' of your Managing Director and will assure you that you can tell him nothing new as he previously worked in your industry (but naturally in a much more senior position to you!). You may catch yourself using terms such as **'big-head'** and **'show-off'** when describing this person.

The Apologist

A tricky category. These people are deemed to be the 'nice' ones. She apologises for troubling you and then apologises for raising a problem. In fact, she apologises for everything! It is easy to relax with The Apologist, falling into a false sense of security and not focusing on resolution, as their apologetic demeanour tricks you into assuming that they will accept a half-hearted resolution. Beware - this is A BIG MISTAKE!

If the Apologist gets as far as complaining, then you *know* she is upset. She may seek to hide the fact, but trust me, she is not happy! If you fall into the trap of delivering an inferior service, then you are in trouble. Just as you complete your call and coo to your colleague, **'She was lovely, I wish they were all like that'**, you can bet that The Apologist is at that moment writing a stinging letter to your Managing Director, raging about your lack of focus.

The Escalator

The Escalator is typified by starting his call logically, speaking slowly and clearly and then building up to an emotional explosion. The errors that can be made here are numerous. This is the type of customer that you quickly transfer to a Supervisor because you just cannot cope with them; and when the Supervisor takes the call, they are completely calm and logical. This is the frustrating situation where your Supervisor comes to you and says, **'I don't know what the fuss was about, he was fine with me.'** More on this is in the **MANAGERS AND LEADERS** chapter.

Timing is of great importance here. Just when you think you have the conversation under control, you put The Escalator on hold. By the time you get back to him, he is screaming again. The feelings of frustration and bewilderment when completing the call can only be eased by copious amounts of coffee and painkillers.

This book cannot go in to the tricks of dealing with every type of difficult caller; however it is my strong belief that all complainants are after the one thing – a resolution. They all have one thing in common – a complaint!

What will be respected most by your caller is not the skill to adapt your style and have a jolly comfortable conversation, but to be someone who actively listens, questions appropriately to fully understand the issue, and then efficiently proceeds to resolution.

CHAPTER FOUR
UNDERSTANDING BEHAVIOURS

In this chapter we are going to explore some of the processes the customer will travel through prior to and during a complaint. It is important this is understood because, as I have said before, the start of the call is all important. We must understand the customer.

We will explore:

- The Complaint Journey
- Escalation of feelings
- Emotion v Logic
- Empathy
- A classic example

The Complaint 'Journey'

Before we embark on the call handling process, I would like you to picture what you are trying to achieve on the journey through a complaint. The ability to understand what is happening for the customer will give you the tools to respond (not react) with the correct skills.

Look at the **COMPLAINT CANYON PICTURE** below. This is a good analogy of what we are attempting to achieve and the journey travelled by the two parties.

There are two areas of land with a deep canyon between them. The only way across this canyon is a very rickety, old bridge. One side of the bridge is the **COMPLAINT** region and the other is the **RESOLUTION.** The rickety bridge is the journey you will be guiding your customer over - a journey that has to be taken by **BOTH PARTIES.**

You, as the complaint handler, are on the **RESOLUTION** side and the customer is stuck firmly on the **COMPLAINT** side... blindfolded!

Your task is to get the customer over to your side of the bridge without looking back, so you are both safely on the **RESOLUTION** side.

This may sound simplistic, but it's a good image. It represents everything we are trying to do when successfully handling complaints.

There are certain steps that must be taken to allow this transition to happen.

The customer cannot navigate the bridge alone, he needs your help. There is little point in you shouting instructions from the resolution side. He does not know the way. (Just as most customers do not know the rules of the regulatory bodies, codes of conduct and consumer protection legislation.)

The first step to be taken is for ***you*** to travel to the customer and join him in the complaint region. You have to experience what it is like on his side of the bridge and understand the customer's feelings and frustrations. They will be varied. Some may be calm and assured. Others will be angry and upset. It is your job to acknowledge and understand those feelings before you can begin assisting with the resolution journey. This is the **EMPATHY** part of complaint handling - acknowledging the feelings.

More on **EMPATHY** later in this chapter.

Once this is explored and you have an understanding of the customer and his frustrations, you will need to explain to him that you are going to take him to the **RESOLUTION** side and how you intend to do it.

This is the part of the complaint call where you only talk about **RESOLUTION**. For the remainder of the interaction, it is the handler's role to keep the journey focussed on **RESOLUTION**.

This is why it is so important to **listen** to the complaint, **empathise, confirm understanding** and then **act**. If you do not do this, your customer will repeatedly return to the complaint because he does not feel heard and understood.

Just like our customer on the bridge, if your customer senses that you do not understand, or you have not explained your intended actions, he will be tempted to return to safe ground, ground he knows... the **COMPLAINT** side.

Assuming that the customer is happy that you fully understand his complaint and you have confirmed that you are going to head towards **RESOLUTION,** then you would metaphorically put your arm around him and lead him to **RESOLUTION.**

As I said before, this is a very basic image but it does represent what we are trying to achieve and how much you can control the call.

OK, with that image in mind we will continue on this journey...

Escalation of 'feelings'

Here is another image for you to digest:

When a customer realises that a product or service is not what they expected, the initial feelings are of FRUSTRATION. This can manifest itself in many ways.

- ***Some people will return or cancel the product or service without comment***
- ***Some will chat to friends over a period of time, expressing their dissatisfaction, and then return or cancel the product or service without comment***
- ***Some will chat to friends over a period of time, expressing their dissatisfaction, and then call to complain***
- ***Some will complain straight away***

Any businessman or woman worth their position would prefer the last of these examples. Remember that the vast majority of dissatisfied customers do not complain. More on this later.

One common theme here in these examples is that the majority of people who complain are just **FRUSTRATED** and disappointed.

If this **FRUSTRATION** is not handled properly at the start of the call, then the customers' feelings will escalate to **ANGER.** This anger can be created by your business long before you get to speak to the customer. Factors that contribute to this are poor websites offering no help, slow transition from dialling a number to speaking with someone, queuing unnecessarily in a shop, and so on.

ANGER IS NOT A FEELING, IT IS A RESPONSE TO A FEELING THE CUSTOMER DOES NOT LIKE. DEAL WITH THE FEELING AND THE ANGER GOES AWAY.

If the **ANGER** is not dealt with, the customer will escalate to **AGGRESSION.** If this is not dealt with then there is one last stage... **VIOLENCE!**

In major conflicts, people will resort to violence when they feel that words are not working. They have run out of skills to communicate verbally and, in an attempt to satisfy their feelings, they resort to physical action. In normal complaint handling, thankfully, this is rare. There is however a sign of violence on the phone. *SLAMMING THE PHONE DOWN*!

On rare occasions, some calls will start with **ANGER** or **AGGRESSION.** These people have wound themselves up to this point before they even make the call. You cannot do anything about this, but your role is the same throughout.

As a front-line call handler, you have little influence over this but your directors do. More on this later too.

The aim is to move the customer back down the scale to SATISFACTION!

Emotion v Logic

This is a very interesting area. The brain is a complex organ and, not being a neuro-scientist, I am in no way qualified to comment on its workings. I can, however, say from experience that there are two major states it can occupy... **EMOTIONAL** and **LOGICAL.**

Unfortunately these two do not mix too well. We engage different parts of the brain for emotion and logic, and the two can not engage together.

When you are emotional, you cannot think logically. How many times have you done or said something when emotional, only to regret it and realise it was a silly or totally illogical thing to say or do when you have 'calmed down' later in the day?

What is happening here is the emotional brain is dominant and takes over. After a while, as the emotion recedes, the logical brain cuts in.

Children are a prime example. Did we not all pack our bags and leave home as a six-year-old, only to regret it by the time we got to the bottom of the garden?

When someone is emotional, attempts at logical communication normally just result in making them MORE emotional and escalate the feelings.

I am sure you have experienced someone speaking emotionally, maybe shouting at you. If your response was something like, **'If you just calm down, I will be able to look up the section and explain it to you'**, you are likely to send the emotional person sky high!

Statements such as **'The law says…'** or **'There is no need to shout…'** will also cause problems. Compliance rules and regulations are NOT to be used unless really necessary. I will explain this further in chapter on **Compliance.**

We must aim to reduce the emotion in the customer and allow the logical brain to take over, before any resolution is embarked upon.

The way we do this is by acknowledging the feelings using EMPATHY.

Empathy

I have realised over the years that many people use the word 'empathy' without really knowing what it means. I have heard numerous definitions and observed many ways of training or coaching the subject.

In recent years I have also heard trainers and business managers stating that **'Empathy is old-fashioned now, we call it...'** They then go on to explain exactly what empathy is but under a different name.

Human behaviour and needs are not fashions, but what they are called and how they are presented in training courses are.

Back to basics – empathy...

I guess it is just one of those subjects that is slightly different for different people.

The Oxford English Dictionary describes it as follows: 'understand and share the feelings of another'. I cannot possibly claim to have the definitive description of empathy in respect of complaint handling, but can pass on to you what works for me and what I have found works for many others.

Empathy is, in its basic form, acknowledging another person's feelings. This is very different from sympathy. Sympathy is very much along the lines of joining in the other person's feelings. It's really pretending to have the same feelings as the other person.

If a person tells you that they did not get the job they had applied for and tell you they are really upset, a good empathetic response would be, **'That must be quite difficult for you.'**

Sympathetic responses to this would be, **'I feel so sorry for you'**, or **'I know exactly what you are feeling right now.'**

I find sympathy, in the context of complaint handling, a very negative and damaging response. My instant reaction to someone who says, **'I know exactly how you feel'**, is **'No, you don't. You do not have a clue how I feel.'**

Be careful with sympathy – it can be dangerous and a touch arrogant!

Back to empathy.

One of the first things we must accept when dealing with complaints, is that all customers see things very differently to you – and this will result in them feeling very different. For example:

Below are two shapes...

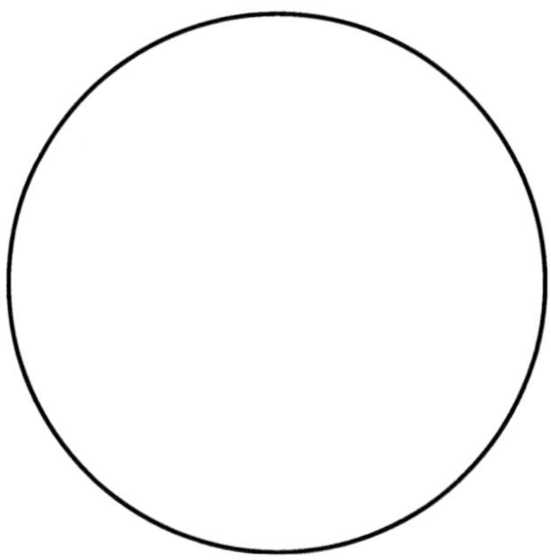

THE CUSTOMER'S VIEW

THE HANDLER'S VIEW

Both parties are looking at very different shapes. The customer clearly sees what is in front of him as a circle. You, as the handler, see it clearly as a rectangle.

The fact is you are looking at the same shape, but from different angles

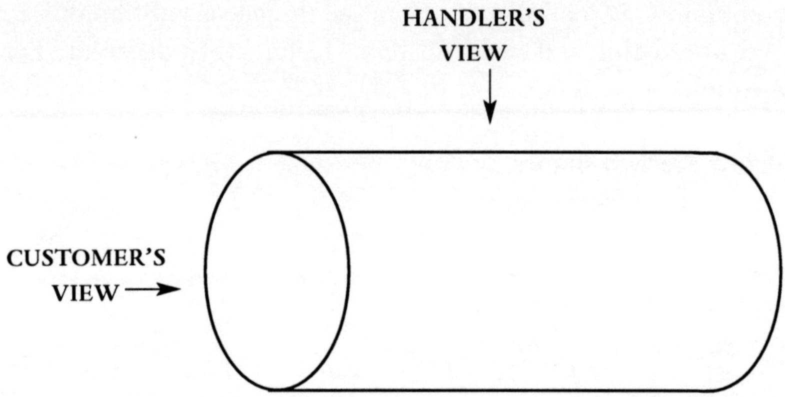

This demonstrates how a complaint could be a run-of-the-mill administration error to you, but could be a very frustrating and upsetting incident for a customer. You must always respect this. People's feelings are never wrong and must be acknowledged even if not understood.

FEELINGS ARE NEVER WRONG. THEY MAY BE BASED ON WRONG OR MISSING INFORMATION, BUT THE FEELING IS NOT WRONG. NEVER TELL A CUSTOMER THAT THEY SHOULD NOT FEEL HOW THEY ARE FEELING.

An example of this could be a customer complaining that his holiday tickets have not arrived and there are only four days to go until they are due to fly.

He pictures standing at the airport with three screaming kids and no tickets.

You picture a pile of tickets on the desk next to you, due to be sent out that day.

Same situation – different views – different information – different feelings!

This all relates to the early part of the call. Remember what we said in earlier chapters? The start of the call is all important and we must acknowledge the customer's feelings before embarking on the resolution.

The following example demonstrates much of this chapter.

Example

Let us look at what may be going on for a customer prior to any call taking place. Remember that the ***'WORLD'S BEST COMPLAINT HANDLER'*** will have no control over this area. This is about human behaviour:

Picture the scene. Caroline has bought a new blouse from a well-known high street outlet, as she has a hot date on Saturday night. She could not resist it; it was in a sale and exactly what she was looking for. She puts it in the wardrobe at home.

The big day arrived. She was working that day and did not have time to get ready until around 6 o'clock. She prepared the ironing board. As she took the blouse out of the bag, she spotted a hole under one arm. She was livid! She looked at the clock and realised the high street shops were closed. **'Oh well, I will have to wear another one and take it back on Monday in my lunch break,'** she thought.

Disappointed, she got ready and went out.

For the whole evening she was annoyed by what had happened. She was looking at other people in their brand new outfits and felt really fed-up. She mentioned her experience to a couple of people, including the name of the shop where she bought her blouse.

On the Sunday, she folded the garment up and placed it back into the bag with the original receipt, ready to take back on the Monday. She was still niggled.

As one o'clock lunchtime arrived on Monday, she started walking to the store. She was thinking to herself…

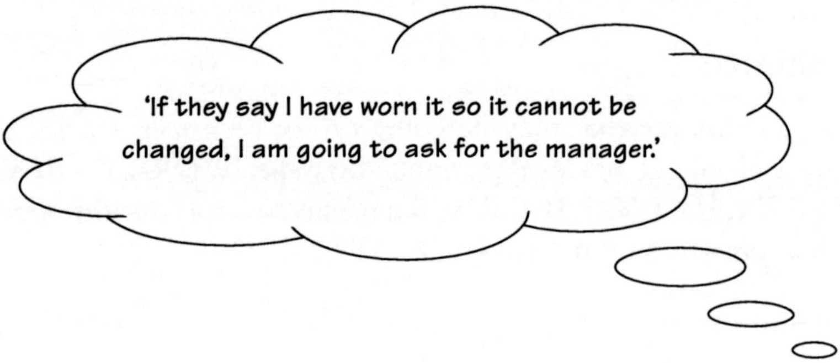

She walked slightly quicker with this thought.

She was now slightly out of breath and muttered a bit louder. She was very frustrated.

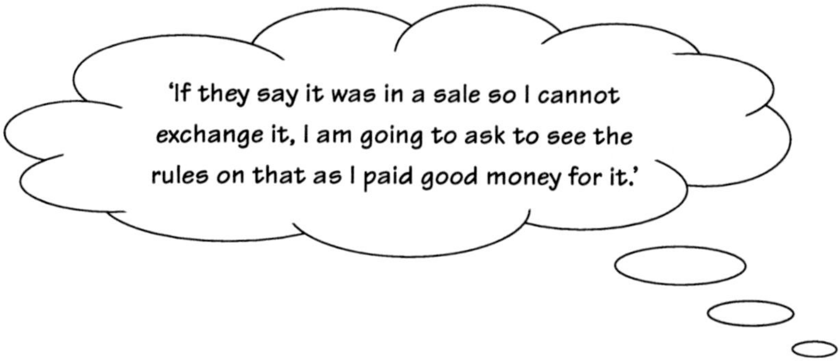

She thought of the money she paid.

The thoughts were coming thick and fast now as she approached the shop. She was anticipating a fight. She had rehearsed all possible defences to her complaint. She had rehearsed to herself her opening line. She is ready, armed and dangerous!

This thought pattern happens in exactly the same way when a customer is hanging on the phone listening to that so-called calming music that your company plays to them.

She arrived at the customer service desk, slightly breathless, heart pumping a little faster than usual, and red in the face.

The assistant was talking to a friend on the phone and arranging a night out. She did not acknowledge Caroline at all, in fact she turned away talking deeper into the phone.

Caroline was now ***ANGRY!***

'Hello, Madam, can I help you,' came the cheery tone of the assistant as she completes her call.

Caroline started talking in clipped tones, separating each word very clearly.

'Yes. I – bought – this – blouse – last – week! It was for a very important night out. When I took it out the bag to wear it, it had this hole in it.'

She put the blouse on the desk, pointing firmly to the offending hole.

She took her hand away, looked at the assistant accusingly and awaited a reply. All of her well-rehearsed defences flashed through her mind. She was ready for battle. She took a small step back.

After what seemed an eternity but was, in fact, just a momentary pause, the assistant replied.

'That must have been awful for you. Let me see what I can do to help you here,' she said, gathering up the garment, bag and receipt.

Caroline was taken aback. In fact she had to pause. She was not expecting that. She was prepared for a battle that clearly was not going to happen. She felt like she had served a ball over a tennis net and the opponent did not hit it back. She was no longer angry but still **FRUSTRATED,** because she did not have a resolution.

Her feelings were acknowledged in the comment ***'That must have been awful for you',*** and the complaint was potentially being turned into a resolution in the line ***'Let me see what I can do to help you here'.***

The assistant returned from the back of the shop.

'I have just checked and, even though it was reduced in the sale, I can refund the money you actually paid in cash or provide you with a credit note for its full pre-sale value to be used in any of our stores.'

Caroline considered the options offered. She had forgotten about her negative feelings and was thinking logically about the resolution. Caroline regularly used the store, so the offers seemed fair and appropriate. She was happy with the response from the assistant and agreed to the credit note.

When Caroline returned to work, her friends asked how she got on.

'Fine,' she said. **'No arguments at all.'**

I am not trying to pretend that all complaints are as straightforward as this, but there are some elements to it that need to be explored.

(1) Caroline wound herself up prior to the visit.
(2) She was uncharacteristically curt and abrupt at the start of the visit. She was not speaking as she normally would. She had predicted a fight. This is no different to people waiting on a phone line. Caroline had a **PERCEPTION!**
(3) Her feelings escalated from **FRUSTRATION** to **ANGER** when she felt unacknowledged.
(4) The very first signal the assistant gave to Caroline was that there was not going to be a fight on this issue. **EMPATHY** was used effectively to acknowledge Caroline's feelings.

(5) Once Caroline's negative feelings were acknowledged, they receded. She had been heard and understood. As soon as the emotional level had lowered, she was able to use logic to consider her options (when she thought about the credit note and her past business with the store). The assistant gave Caroline **REALITY** and her **PERCEPTION** went away.

PERCEPTION DOES NOT EXIST WHERE THERE IS REALITY

(6) The assistant only spoke about the resolution. This is important. Once the feelings and frustration of the complainant have been acknowledged by good empathetic responses, the conversation should only be about the resolution - not the complaint. The complaint should be put in the past and left there.

Although this is a face-to-face example, it does display many of the characteristics of how a person complaining can change when a good complaint handler uses the right skills in the right order.

THE CUSTOMER HAS THE COMPLAINT –
YOU **HAVE THE RESOLUTION!**

CHAPTER FIVE
COMPLIANCE AND REGULATION

We are living in a world dominated by compliance requirements, regulations, codes of conduct and internal rules. These are usually in place for very good reasons and most of them, believe it or not, are designed to protect the customer.

For example, time deadlines dictated by these rules are in place to ensure that customers are not ignored and that unprofessional companies can be held to account or even prohibited from trading. I have no issues with regulation and support the focus they generate.

These rules only become a problem when they are applied or referred to needlessly. This is very common at all levels of an organisation and must be addressed.

The rules and deadlines set by regulatory authorities should be regarded as irrelevant when it comes to customer service. Just because all of a company's output or administration falls 'within the rules' does NOT indicate that it is good service. It just indicates that you are not breaking the rules.

I once went to a business where the management were very proud that they answer all complaint correspondence within **'the 21 days allowed'**. I looked into this and the average response time from receiving a customer letter (or e-mail) to acknowledging it was 19 days! Terrible service, but the managers of the company were delighted.

Further investigation revealed that out of 132 letters, 117 had either written again in this period or called to chase a response. These responses were received by a different department so were not cross-referenced. The management had NO IDEA of the expense and bad reputation their company was getting. It was, however, very, very proud that it was **'within service standards'**.

Regulatory deadlines are NOT service standards – they are worst case deadlines.

When it comes to handling a complaint, I shudder when I hear compliance and regulations mentioned. Very often, if the advisor or shop assistant is unsure or not trained, he will fall back on these rules to try and 'handle' the complaint. Dangerous ground.

Look back at the example in the introduction to this book. When Mrs Clarke is transferred to Jane in Customer Service, Jane responds to her request with,

'By law we have 28 days to issue adjustments.'

This is a typical example of using compliance in an attempt to handle a call.

To be frank – it should never be mentioned. Just because you have 28 days, it does not mean you have to use it. It also does not mean that responding in 20 days is good.

Set your own service standards and set them to be within the parameters of how your customers WANT TO BE TREATED, rather than how the regulatory bodies say is the minimum standard.

Train your staff to use their skills and not rules.

The rules are there for a reason - that reason is not to be used to handle a call.

Internal rules must not hinder the call handler resolving complaints. I will explore this more in later chapters.

CHAPTER SIX
CALL SKILLS AND RESOLUTIONS

Now we need to look at the ideal structure of a call. This is not set in stone and of course every call will be different, but hopefully by now you can see that handling difficult calls in a methodical manner with the right skills can avoid that needless escalation of feelings.

OPENING
LISTEN BUT DO NOT JUDGE

EMPATHY
EMPATHISE AND MOVE ON

QUESTIONING
SEEK INFORMATION

SUMMARY
CLARIFYING UNDERSTANDING

COMPLAINT/RESOLUTION JUNCTION
DISCUSS ONLY RESOLUTION FROM NOW ON

RESOLUTION
AGREEMENT ON ACTIONS

CLOSE

This is the ideal call flow – let's look in some detail…

THE OPENING

There is no way that the handler can know how long the customer has been harbouring this complaint. It could be two minutes or it could have been on their mind for several weeks. They may be ready to scream at you or talk calmly right from the outset.

We cannot assume or predict any of this.

Be aware of your own emotional state. You may have just dealt with a very difficult call and you may not be in an ideal state of mind to receive another. Ensure this is not reflected in your opening statements.

Don't forget that it is far easier to change your behaviour (how you sound on the phone) than your attitude (the reality of how you feel).

YOUR ATTITUDE AFFECTS YOUR BEHAVIOUR
YOUR BEHAVIOUR AFFECTS THE CUSTOMER'S ATTITUDE
THE CUSTOMER'S ATTITUDE AFFECTS CUSTOMER'S BEHAVIOUR
THE CUSTOMER'S BEHAVIOUR AFFECTS YOUR ATTITUDE
AND SO ON

This can be a downward spiral or, preferably, with helpful and willing behaviour from you, it will increase the comfort of the call on both sides.

- As the phone rings, there is one person in your life for the foreseeable future: the customer.
- This customer must be treated as if they are the only customer you have spoken to or will be speaking to that day.

IN BUSINESS THERE IS NOTHING MORE IMPORTANT THAN A CUSTOMER COMPLAINT!

- If you are in a face-to-face situation and happen to be dealing with someone else or on the phone, acknowledge the customer, even if it is just with a smile. Let them know that you know they are there.
- If you are answering the phone, please ensure that the customer cannot hear the last part of your conversation with your colleagues. There is nothing worse than a customer hearing,

'Hang on, Sandra, I will just take this call... Good Morning, Paynton Publishing, how can I help you?'

- Open the call with a smile. Your voice is a powerful tool, use it. You really can hear a smile. A cheerful reception may avoid the escalation of 'feelings'.
- Take ownership of the call. Rather than say 'we' and 'us', use 'I' and 'me'. When things get tough during a call, we tend to revert to 'we' and 'us'. Be aware of this. As soon as you are speaking on behalf of a large organisation, you become impersonal. This allows the customer false comfort to say things that they would not to an individual and can actually encourage aggression. It is easier for a customer to say, **'Your company is a bunch of sharks'** than it is for them to say, **'You are a shark'.**
- Your customer may mention how long she has been waiting for you to take her call. It is perfectly proper to apologise here, but rather than give a reason, just repeat, **'How can I help?'** and maybe repeat your name again and move the call on.

IF THE SERVICE IS GOOD ENOUGH AT THE END OF A QUEUE, THE WAIT WILL BE FORGOTTEN

LISTEN BUT DO NOT JUDGE

- Once you have opened the conversation, listen actively. Use 'verbal nods'. These are phrases such as 'OK', 'I see' or relevant acknowledgement noises that show you are listening but *do not interrupt.*
- As the customer is talking, take notes if you can. Try not to prejudge the resolution at this stage. Even if you know the resolution, please, please, please do not interrupt the customer while they are telling their story. You may have heard it a thousand times, but it is their first - and hopefully only - time.

'Yes, yes, Mr Smith, I know what you are going to say and I can deal with it now.'

This may sound efficient, but does nothing for the blood pressure of your customers.

- Remember what we will need to do soon – EMPATHISE. We need to listen to how our customer feels and recognise the detail of the *REAL* problem.

MANY COMPLAINTS THAT REACH HEAD OFFICE ARE NOT ABOUT WHAT MADE THE PERSON COMPLAIN IN THE FIRST PLACE, BUT MORE ABOUT THE WAY THEY WERE TREATED WHILE COMPLAINING!

- Treat customers well at this point and you will have a good chance of satisfying them, even if you do not resolve the issue.

EMPATHISE AND MOVE ON

- Once your customer has opened the call and explained her position, you can empathise where required.
- **'Sorry to hear you felt that way, Mrs Peters, that must have been a real problem for you at the time. Let me see what I can do to help you. I will need to ask you a few questions, is that OK?'** This would be a good empathetic approach. This also takes control of the call.
- Customers will sometimes continue talking about the complaint. This is simply because they do not feel as though you have understood their feelings or empathised enough. Try again to listen and empathise.
- Good practice, when using empathetic statements, is immediately follow them up with the **'Let me see if I can help you'** type of statement. This assists you in keeping control of the call and moving on from complaint to resolution.
- To some customers, empathy is just permission to keep moaning! The call will turn into a very negative one if *YOU* as the complaint handler do not turn it around to show you want to get on with assisting them.

Remember...

Empathise and suggest moving on without a pause, using the words RESOLUTION or RESOLVE!

QUESTIONING

- If you asked the customer for permission to ask a few questions and indicated why (to understand the complaint), you will find that he is usually comfortable to answer you. This is called SIGNPOSTING. The customer must be directed here. Go back to the vision of taking the person over the bridge.
- Two good types of questions are **CLOSED** and **DIRECTIONAL.**
- You will all know closed questions I am sure. These are questions that are very direct and encourage single word answers: **'When did you receive the letter, Mr Johnson?'** or **'What colour is the bike that was delivered, Mrs Jones?'**
- You may notice I am using the customer's name a lot. This is always good practice as it helps to build relations with the customer and reflects you taking personal interest.

- If permission has been given and you have indicated your desire to help, then most customers are happy to be questioned this way.
- You may experience a customer who wants to tell you her life story. Your simple question, **'What time did the delivery person arrive, Mrs Blackwell?'** often produces a response along the lines of…

  'Well, it was Thursday morning; I know it was Thursday as I was due to meet Doris at the club for lunch. No, it was Wednesday. It was Wednesday, wasn't it Harry? Because Doris cancelled that week as her son, Martin, went to her house to mend the boiler on the Thursday…'
- We have all been there and they can be difficult to handle. I would suggest **DIRECTIONAL** questions. These questions dictate what style of answer you require. The clue is in the question and they are very effective.

  'Could you tell me <u>*briefly*</u> what happened please, Mr Jackman?'

  'Could you please tell me <u>*exactly*</u> what price were you quoted, Mrs Cross?'
- This helps keep the control with you. Remember, the customer has no idea of the level of detail you require. Subconsciously, customers find these questions very helpful.

I would like to raise a couple of points on open questioning. I have attended courses and read copious quantities of material about questioning techniques. I find it irritating that trainers introduce the differences between **OPEN** and **CLOSED** questions, and then spend the vast majority of the time training only **OPEN** questions with a derisory allocation of time on **CLOSED** questions.

Closed questioning is a major skill in itself. Closed questions are used for getting specific information very efficiently. You will have less need for **OPEN** questioning as, certainly while the complaint is being explained, it may not be a great idea to explore the depth of feeling and personal anguish too deeply!

As long as you asked permission to question and obtained the customer's consent, then *YOU* will relax and the *CUSTOMER* will relax, safe in the knowledge that you are trying to gain *CLARITY* and ultimately assist the customer.

'OK, Mrs Smith, I need to ask you a few questions to establish exactly what the problem is. Is that OK?'

A word of warning here. Try not to ask more than three questions without some kind of break, otherwise it sounds like you are filling in a form. Ask three questions and then say statements such as, **'Thanks for that, I am getting this clear now'** *then* continue with the questions.

CLARIFYING

Also known as summarising.

- Once you have questioned fully, it is vital that you repeat back to your customer your *EXACT* understanding of the problem. There is nothing worse than assuming and then solving only part of the issue.
- If you do this, the feelings will escalate and you will have a worse problem than when you started.
- Repeat back and get approval that you have got under the skin of the issue.
- Many complaint customers will have more than one issue. After summarising, make sure you ask if there are any other issues before you go on to resolution. This is a bit like filling

a 'shopping basket'. Going back to the complaint in chapter one, Jane should have asked for all of the issues before progressing to transferring Dot.

- If you do not do this and successfully solve what you think is the whole problem, the customer may say, **'OK, thanks for that. I now have another problem!'** This will escalate 'feelings'; unfortunately this time they will be *YOURS!*
- When clarifying, a customer will very often give you clues to what a satisfactory resolution would be. When you repeat the complaint back to the customer, it is the first time the customer has heard it from another voice. They will often listen to it and may say statements such as, **'Yes, that's it, and all I want is a refund'**, or **'Yes, that is the problem and nobody has apologised once'.**

LISTEN TO YOUR CUSTOMERS - THEY OFTEN GIVE YOU THE COMPLAINT *AND* THE RESOLUTION.

COMPLAINT/RESOLUTION JUNCTION

- Once summarised and agreement has been reached, you need to signpost that you are moving on to the resolution. You are now starting the journey over the bridge.
- Good quotes here may be, **'OK, Mr Patterson, now I understand the issue and I am going to see how I can resolve it'**, or **'Thanks, Mrs Evans, let me see how I can resolve this now'.**

NOW LEAVE THE COMPLAINT WHERE IT IS!

- The words **RESOLVE** and **RESOLUTION** are all-powerful here.
- It is now your responsibility to ensure you keep the conversation on **RESOLUTION** and not the **COMPLAINT**. After all, if you were going across the rickety bridge, you would not keep running back to the wrong side.
- Progress as smoothly as possible in one direction.
- The customer may be tempted to keep mentioning the complaint. If you have empathised and summarised properly this will not happen much, but if it does, remind the customer that you are seeking a **RESOLUTION**. They normally accept this readily.
- The customer may want to keep going back – they are unsure of the rickety bridge – they do not know how you are going to resolve this situation. Reassure them, repeat that you are trying to resolve the situation.
- Sometimes you have to be quite firm, '**OK, Mr Smith, that is the complaint. I really want to resolve this and we can do a "post mortem" on why it happened afterwards.**' Very often the post mortem is forgotten if the resolution is satisfactory.

DO NOT REVISIT THE COMPLAINT YOURSELF – DO NOT KEEP APOLOGISING FOR IT – YOU ARE ONLY TRYING TO MAKE YOURSELF FEEL BETTER!

REMEMBER – YOU HAVE THE RESOLUTION NOT THE COMPLAINT!

HOLD AND WAIT SKILLS

Many resolutions will require you to refer to another person or documents in another area of the business. Putting someone on hold or asking them to wait for you is a skill in itself. There are three vital elements to this process:

- Say what you will be doing
- Tell the customer how long you are going to be
- Ask permission

'Mrs Pardew, I need to check with Distribution to see when they can re-deliver. I will be about three minutes, is that OK?'

Once this is done, YOU and the CUSTOMER can relax. The customer has given you permission. They have taken the option to wait. They may decide to continue with their work and put the phone on loud speaker; they may just sit back in the chair and relax. Whatever it is, permission has been given. This keeps you relaxed.

If it transpires that you are going to take longer, please go back to the customer and inform them and gain more permission.

When you are busy, time goes quickly, when you are holding on a line listening to dour 'hold music', it drags, believe me, try it!

RESOLUTIONS

This is a difficult area to go into any detail. Companies have their own ideas about resolution.

Some will focus primarily on customer satisfaction and rely heavily on word of mouth to attract other customers. They need to ensure total satisfaction with complaint handling.

Some companies will not give quite as much focus and see a resolution as the customer going away with minimal damage to the company's reputation.

There is not a right or wrong level of attention given to complaints. A board of directors must decide on the correct focus to support the company vision and overall strategy to achieve it.

Compliance is a major area of concern here. Compliance simply gives a framework to work within, it does not necessarily mean that full adherence to it will resolve more complaints.

I can only touch on some general principles and skills.

TO RESOLVE OR NOT TO RESOLVE?

One of the first considerations is whether you actually want to resolve a problem in the first place.

It could be company policy to receive a few complaints about a particular aspect of the business, rather than spend unmanageable amounts of money changing the problem.

An example of this could be automatically sending receipts for telephone payments. A company may have a policy of only sending receipts when requested. This may generate 200 calls a year with people complaining they did not receive a receipt (they had not requested one). A company may deem it better to handle those 200 calls per year and log the complaints rather than spend £150,000 issuing receipts to ALL customers, most of whom simply dispose of them.

RESOLUTION AGREED

Once a RESOLUTION has been agreed between the customer and the handler, confirm with the customer clearly:

- What you will be doing
- What they have to do
- What they do not have to do

For example:

'Mr Gordon, I am going to issue another form to you today, first class, to 23 Acacia Drive, Plumford, Essex. You do not have to complete it again. Simply sign it and send it back to me personally in the pre–paid envelope, and I will ensure it is dealt with.'

It may be your company policy to follow up all resolutions in writing. Notice, I use the word resolution and not complaint! Ensure the letter follows similar principles.

THERE IS NO RESOLUTION?

Some complaints seemingly have no resolution. These can be misperceptions by the customer or just mistakes by the company that cannot be resolved.

A common and difficult one may be, **'You have written to my husband. He died three years ago. How do you think that made me feel?'**

This seemingly has no resolution. Think about it though, the customer must know it has no resolution. It cannot be undone.

The customer knows that. What would satisfy the customer? What are they calling for? Do they just want an acknowledgement of their feelings? Do they want an apology?

These calls often make complaint handlers freeze. Talk to the customer, empathise, apologise, ensure that it cannot happen again and confirm with the customer what steps you have taken to stop it happening.

People may complain about price increases, or they do not like the new company logo. In these cases it is important to deliver an empathetic call and apology.

You can only hope that in time, when heightened emotions subside for the customer, they may think, **'Well, they did at least apologise.'**

Very often you will hear a customer say, **'I just wanted an apology.'**

I would not be surprised if many complaints are satisfactorily resolved with simple empathy and a genuine apology.

If there was no error made and the customer is simply mistaken, it is perfectly acceptable to apologise that they feel the way they do. You are NOT apologising for an error. Do not be tempted to keep repeating, **'It is not our fault'**, or **'In fact, Mr Edwards, you are wrong on this'.**

It serves no purpose, apart from making you feel better!

RESOLUTION NOT ACCEPTABLE

Sometimes you will not be able to deliver the type of resolution the customer really requires. It is simply not feasible. On these occasions you will need to deliver the news sensitively. Whenever you say you cannot do something, it is always good practice to follow up with what you can do.

'I am afraid I cannot arrange delivery for tomorrow, but I can arrange it for Thursday at a time convenient for you.'

If there are not *any* options available for resolution, then the best way forward is similar to the above where you can say something along the lines:

'I am sorry but I cannot send the knife set to you as the stock is completely gone and there are no plans for a further delivery. What I can do is apologise on behalf of Cuisine Bits Ltd that your order was missed.'

This will probably not satisfy the customer's feelings immediately and the best you can hope for is that, following the call, the customer may resign himself or herself to the fact you tried and you apologised.

You may have some occasions where you have suggested your only possible resolution and the customer repeatedly says it is not acceptable. She keeps returning to the complaint and explaining that the resolution just does not work for her. This call has reached a stalemate. The customer is not accepting the resolution at all.

If your resolution is truly the only possible option and you have thoroughly explored all avenues, you need to give that customer the message.

There is a technique which requires skill and confidence in these areas.

If you offer your resolution, clearly such as:

'I am afraid I cannot arrange delivery on Christmas Eve, but I can do any day during the week running up to it.'

The customer protests.

You repeat the exact same words and exact tone.

'I am afraid I cannot arrange delivery on Christmas Eve, but I can do any day during the week running up to it.'

The customer may protest again.

Again you repeat. This is called the 'broken record' technique for obvious reasons.

'I am afraid I cannot arrange delivery on Christmas Eve, but I can do any day during the week running up to it.'

Rarely will you have to repeat this more than three times. The customer will realise that you have explored all options and this is the only resolution on offer.

This technique comes with a health warning though – it should only be used in extreme circumstances.

AGREE RESOLUTIONS - AVOID IMPOSING

Where possible always try to ***agree*** the resolutions with the customer. Sometimes there is more than one option. Give the customer the choice. This transfers part of the ownership of the resolution to them and aids overall satisfaction.

Listen hard – the customer will often give clues for a resolution which is often less than you may think.

It may be that you cannot resolve the issue there and then. On these occasions, tell the customer what actions you will be taking, what they have to do, what they do not have to do and all relevant time-scales.

CLOSE

This is such a common area for problems. You need to be very disciplined here.

You have invested a lot of time and effort on your call to arrive at your agreed resolution. You have opened the call well, you have listened, empathised, summarised, moved the call to resolution, concentrated on the resolution, confirmed the resolution steps and then you say, **'OK, Mr Davis, apologies once again for the error!'**

NO! NO! NO! NO! NO! NO! NO! NO!

You **do not** return the customer back to the complaint. This is just showing off. You are subconsciously reminding the customer that they had a complaint and you resolved it. This is only massaging your ego and has no place in good customer service.

When taking the customer across the bridge and you are three feet from the RESOLUTION side, you would not run them all the way back.

Finish the call in resolution and ensure only the resolution is spoken about when the call is completed.

There is no further need to apologise. If you have empathised and apologised properly at the start and the customer is happy you are working for them, then the complaint should be left where it belongs – **IN THE PAST!**

YOU ARE HANDLING A RESOLUTION - NOT A COMPLAINT!

REPORTING

A vital area for all businesses is improvement. I said earlier that the best and cheapest form of customer research is customer complaints. Your company should have adequate reporting function.

It is very easy to forget the reporting side, as often calls stimulate feelings in the agent that results in them losing focus immediately after the call. These feelings could be positive if they had a good call, or negative if it was a particularly difficult one.

This may result in the complaint not being recorded. If the complaints are not recorded, they cannot be analysed. If they are not analysed, there will be no improvement. If there is no improvement, the complaints continue.

The whole methodology of reporting and analysing complaints is not a subject for this book, but I feel it is important to raise its profile.

Here is a reminder of the call structure:

OPENING
LISTEN BUT DO NOT JUDGE

EMPATHY
EMPATHISE AND MOVE ON

QUESTIONING
SEEK INFORMATION

SUMMARY
CLARIFYING UNDERSTANDING

COMPLAINT/RESOLUTION JUNCTION
DISCUSS ONLY RESOLUTION FROM NOW ON

RESOLUTION
AGREEMENT ON ACTIONS

CLOSE

CHAPTER SEVEN
COMPENSATION

The whole subject of compensation must be taken very seriously. It is generally perceived that we are living now in a 'compensation society'. It is often thought that people are actively seeking opportunities to claim compensation.

If you tell a friend that you tripped in the street, the instant response is often, **'You want to go for compensation there.'**

I am not going to argue the 'compensation society' point here. What I will say is that, from experience, a huge amount of compensation payments are made totally unnecessarily and serve little purpose in successful complaint and resolution handling.

To explain this point, I will give you another scenario. A customer makes a complaint to a satellite TV company. She is not getting all the channels she has ordered and is paying for. Her first call did not conclude with any resolution. Her second call also failed to get a satisfactory response. She writes in to the company but gets no reply and her e-mails do not get answered.

Eventually the customer calls to cancel the product. The call handler is experienced in these matters, as he is working in the department trained to try and keep customers. By now the customer is so upset that her complaint has not been resolved, her mind has gone to how much it has cost her to follow up this error. She is getting angry.

At the start of the call to the experienced handler, she relays the problem and then ADDS ON the demand for compensation for her time, calls and postage.

Now let us pause here. The time, calls and postage may add up to just a few pounds (although many people demand hundreds). If that handler immediately sends a cheque in the post, will the customer think, **'OK, that's good, they really are**

a good company. They really know how to handle complaints and are top notch when it comes to customer service?'

I don't think so – in fact, from experience, I have found that demands for compensation are often a 'cry for help', an attempt to try and get a good quality response from the handler. Especially when the customer feels that they are not being taken seriously.

It is almost in the same bracket as...

- 'I want to speak to your manager'
- 'I am going to go to Watchdog'
- 'I want compensation'
- 'I will report you to the Law Society'
- 'My MP will be hearing about this'

Can you see how neatly it fits in?

Compensation comes to most people's minds when they are dissatisfied with how the complaint has been handled, NOT about the failure of the product or service in the first place.

It is odd to see that, as employees progress up the management ladder in many organisations, their budgets and authority to sanction payments to customers increases. I would say that is directly linked to the escalation of complaints.

If the complaint has escalated as far as, say, Supervisor level, then the frustration and anger have increased to the extent that compensation is being asked for, but not to an excessive degree. It would not be justified, as the number of calls and time engaged should not have amounted to justify a large payment.

If the complaint continues to be unresolved here and it escalates further 'up the management ladder' all the way to the Managing Director's desk, then the chances are the customer has sought independent advice and a fully justified claim for a large compensation payment is on the table.

This is why the budgets or 'permissions to pay' increase as the status of the role increases.

Even if compensation is paid – what job has it done? All it has done is acknowledged the company's ***poor service*** – it does not indicate ***good service.***

You cannot buy loyalty.

Once a customer has got to the point of having to ask for compensation, she has immediately increased her own expectations. They now want to see the matter resolved ***AND*** receive compensation.

In many respects, once compensation is demanded it is difficult to fully satisfy the customer. Don't forget – compensation is not a resolution!

I have had experiences where, at the start of the call, when the customer is explaining the complaint, they get so 'worked up' that the demands for compensation appear at this early stage. Let me explain how to deal with this.

As mentioned earlier, at the start of the call the customer's brain is very much engaged in its 'emotional' state. Things are said that may not be logical. A simple complaint that a customer only got 19 biscuits in a 20 biscuit pack, when explained, can lead up to the accusation that it totally ruined a family picnic and the company **'should pay for the petrol there and back'**.

It is your job to focus on the complaint at this stage and establish exactly what the problem is – do not, at this stage argue the compensation demand. Try not to refer to it (no matter how ridiculous the demand is). Continue, as advised, in confirming understanding of the complaint and lead on to resolution.

By now the customer will possibly be more logical and reasonable. Many times the compensation issue will be forgotten. If not, and you have resolved the complaint correctly, the grounds for compensation will be minimised and the customer will realise that a claim for compensation is impractical.

What often happens is when a handler hears a claim for compensation at this stage (not realising it's a cry for help), they immediately refuse or say, **'That is ridiculous; one biscuit does not spoil a picnic.'** This is so unhelpful and, if such statements are made when the customer is in 'emotional mind', their state of frustration or anger jumps up to aggression very, very quickly.

This will also make the customer 'dig their heels in' and will not let the matter lie.

Training and supporting the 'front line' call handlers of customer-facing staff will dramatically reduce the complaints that lead to these calls for compensation.

The next chapter, Management and Leaders, explores the area of support and training in more detail.

CHAPTER EIGHT
MANAGERS AND LEADERS

Strong leadership is key to the whole success of creating a world class customer service area. Attitudes and approaches on the 'front line' of any business are moulded and developed from good quality leadership and management.

However, when I have been invited into businesses to explore the potential to minimise complaints and reduce compensation payments, I have discovered that most of the problems originate from poor management.

It is very common in business that the people with the simplest and most effective ideas are found in two areas - the very top of the management tree (CEO, MD etc), and the 'front line' (advisors and shop assistants).

The bit in the middle gets complex, political and can rapidly lose sight of the customer.

In many companies, the first step in the line of career progression from a customer-facing role upwards is often a Team Leader or Supervisor. Employees who make this progression are probably ambitious and want to get involved in other aspects of the business. This is quite natural.

Just to diversify a little here. If Leadership and Management are the only line of progression provided for people to enhance their income and status, then the organisation may be creating a leadership line wholly unsuited to the task.

For example – you have a very good sales person, or a person who is a great ambassador for quality customer service. These employees are a wonderful example to their peers and a great asset to the team. You want to retain these people, but they want to progress and increase their income or status within the company, so you promote them along the only line available - leadership or management. They are no longer speaking to customers on the telephone. Have you not just reduced their value to the company? Have you not lessened your options by having such a rigid progression structure?

'Front line' staff thrive on the customer contact and the joy of sales and service. Take them into the world of spreadsheets, presentations and weekly meetings, and often they will lose their enthusiasm and sparkle.

Providing progression for people, while still utilising the skills that made them valuable in the first place, is surely an area to explore?

Back to the advisor who is now promoted to a Team Leader. One of the first things that happens during this progression is the new leader thinks to himself, **'I don't have to be on the phones any more. Great.'** He enters the world of spreadsheets, meetings, wages, budgets, meetings, presentations and meetings. He now has a new set of colleagues around him. He is now a proud member of the 'leaders' club'. He joins the other leaders for social events and attends 'leaders' lunches'.

He is no longer speaking to customers on the telephone, and his painstakingly honed telephone skills begin to lose their sharpness. He may not realise it, but it is happening. It is rather like brakes wearing out on a car. Each day you have to press fractionally harder for the brakes to engage. You do not realise you brakes are getting low until you have new ones fitted and, all of a sudden, you only have to touch the brake to make it work. Only then do you realise how you were compensating for slowly eroding performance.

The perceived value of the new leader is based on the quality of his or her administration and their interaction with higher management. He or she wants to be noticed.

I know this is a massive generalisation but I assure you, in my experience, this is rife in British industry.

As the leader takes on more work (and much of this is self-generated), they get busier and busier. Now they do not have time to speak to customers who demand to speak to a Supervisor. They are too busy to train their team to deal with difficult customers. They do not visit the shop floor as much as they did, or all that can be seen of them is one inch of head above a computer monitor.

The pressures for recruitment, disciplinaries, monitoring sickness, etc, are too great to have the time to speak with customers.

This explains why, when a complaint customer calls demanding to speak with a Supervisor or **'someone with authority'**, he meets with the response, **'Our Supervisors do not speak to customers.'**

As we start to gaze further up the management chain, we often observe senior managers putting pressure on their junior managers to deliver additional tasks within demanding deadlines and therefore positively encouraging the Team Leader and Supervisors NOT to talk to customers.

THERE IS NOTHING MORE IMPORTANT IN A BUSINESS THAN A CUSTOMER COMPLAINT

I said earlier in this book that the complaining customer is the most effective way for getting feedback on the business and how it is viewed from the outside.

Imagine this Senior Management Meeting – two Managers are asked to make a presentation to the CEO on how to improve the weekly adverts that go into the national press.

Manager 1 has consulted the marketing companies, spoken internally with the marketing staff, checked on new product ranges and presents her proposals for a new design.

Manager 2 states that she has spoken to 35 customers in the past two months who have all given very similar feedback and said they would have increased their product purchases if they had known in the advert that a certain product is available.

See the difference? Who is most impressive to the CEO? Above all, **Manager 2** has more accurate information, has developed a great idea for free (no meetings there), and satisfied 35 customers along the way!

Manager 1 has spent ages in meetings, has no hard evidence on which to base her ideas and, worst of all, she has refused to take calls as she is too busy.

Manager 2 has also given a fantastic example to her staff by speaking with these customers.

The whole area of support and training is a difficult one to address, because few companies really want to admit that they have complaints. This is naïve, but very common.

I hope that, by now, you have accepted that 'front line resolution' saves a lot of compensation payments and creates good will and loyalty. Unfortunately accepting that is not enough. Companies must give the 'front line' the tools to do the job.

Training and coaching is a huge investment for any business. Training and coaching complaint handling is extremely rewarding, as the benefits are immediately measurable at all levels of the business. If the training is successful, very soon you will see fewer complaints escalate and a lower demand for compensation payments.

Where the businesses often go wrong and stifle the training is in the area of empowerment. Senior management are often very cautious about giving any authority to the people actually speaking to customers. The authority to refund, exchange goods or pay compensation often starts at Team Leader level (to a small degree), and the authority levels increase as you travel up the management ladder.

I have heard the assumption made that if the 'front line' staff were to be given the authority to make payments, they would agree to anything just to calm the customer down, and payments would escalate. I disagree with this.

The following is a common scenario. A complaint call is received by an advisor. Two payments have been taken out of a customer's direct debit in error. They do NOT have the authority to agree that the payment is returned immediately, only the Team Leader can do that. She is not available. The customer is now angry and is shouting at the advisor demanding resolution. The advisor is stuck.

Five hours pass and the Team Leader eventually calls the customer and agrees the payment. The customer is now satisfied and does not vent her anger at the Team Leader. An inexperienced Team Leader then goes to the advisor and complains, **'I don't know what you were fussing about. She was OK with me.'**

How does that advisor feel? What is the organisation telling her about her worth?

How does the customer feel? What is the view of that advisor when she had to say, **'I do not have the authority'**?

Many business leaders are sitting at their desks at this moment with a pile of customer complaints demanding compensation and threatening court action, because they have not got the courage or structure to give empowerment to the members of staff actually speaking with customers.

It is not a difficult task to train people to use this empowerment properly. Reward and recognition structures can manage how much it is used and Team Leaders can monitor anybody using this in place of skills.

Very tight controls on empowerment are put in place to save money – often when analysed, they cost a lot more money in the long run and cost a lot more than money in bad reputation for delaying financial resolutions.

CHAPTER NINE
SUMMARY

Most complaints that escalate as far as the Director's desk are not about the original complaint itself. Not many of these complaints will be about goods being delivered to the wrong address, or too many knots in the wood the company supplied.

The complaints that get to this level are normally about the *service* the customer received when they did complain.

Very often the customer is so aggrieved that there are now claims for compensation for time taken and postage, etc. This in itself can be expensive without considering the amount of time a Director will have to take responding to the complainant.

Many complaints go to governing bodies and regulatory authorities. These are often along the same lines.

The whole subject of complaint handling is all too often neglected.

When you assess the time and effort taken to resolve the issues at a higher level, by which time the frustrated customer has grown to be very angry, you will realise how much that lack of focus is costing you in **FINANCIAL** and **REPUTATION** terms.

I have already mentioned how customers will be more likely to stick with a company where a previous complaint was handled well. In fact, many *increase* their product density with that particular company. It could be said that...

Hearing customer complaints is a positive thing and should be encouraged. It is far better to hear the complaint yourself than someone else!

A disturbing thought for many people? Consider this:

Good handling can positively encourage further loyalty and product sales.

Only a very small percentage of customers with a problem actually complain.

Isn't it obvious that we should actively encourage those who have a complaint, and don't call, to pick up the phone?

The art of good complaint handling is all in the first contact. This is where the real skills apply. This is where the potential escalation in the gravity of the complaint can be managed.

In my experience, the very highest level of management in an organisation usually understands this, as do the call handlers and customer assistants. The biggest breakdown tends to be with Supervisors, Team Leaders and 'middle management'. They do not like handling complaints and do not see the added value a well handled issue can be to a business.

Ask yourself this – how many of the agendas in your management or team meetings have **COMPLAINTS** mentioned on them? If they do, are they at the top or wallowing down near **ANY OTHER BUSINESS**?

My theory, and the very basis of this book, is to avoid escalation by enabling the call handlers and customer assistants to settle the complaints with the right skills and high levels of personal empowerment.

I will leave you with a quick story of something that happened to me personally.

I bought a toy for my young daughter from a large high street supermarket. I had reason to return the toy as it was damaged. I entered the store with my daughter and looked for assistance. I found a lady on the 'twilight shift' stacking a shelf with Cream Crackers. The exchange went as follows.

'I wonder if you can help me, I bought this toy yesterday and it is damaged,' I said in a measured voice. I was a bit niggled, as I would rather have been eating my dinner.

'Certainly I can help you,' said the assistant, instantly discarding her job.

'What is your name?' she said to my daughter.

Once they had exchanged names, the assistant took us directly to the area where the toys were. She offered me a replacement or my money back. Just as I was going to agree to the refund, my daughter agreed a replacement!

Quietly the assistant said to me, **'Is your daughter allowed some sweets?'**

I confirmed that was OK. At this point the assistant reached into her apron, signed off two £1 vouchers from a chequebook-type pad, passed them to my daughter with a cheery, **'Have some sweets on me.'**

Off we went, totally satisfied and eager to eat.

I reflected on this situation over dinner and noted a few points.

1. I was not passed to anyone else
2. The assistant instantly stopped what she was doing and focussed 100% on us
3. She offered alternative resolutions
4. She had vouchers actually in her pocket; she signed them off without referring to anyone else

I am in no way deriding the position of a twilight assistant, but it is not known as the highest level of management. If ***she*** has voucher books in her pocket, does that mean ***everyone*** has? It must.

Total empowerment, total skills… total bliss!

CHAPTER TEN
DOT AND DEREK REVISITED

I thought it worthwhile to look at the example of the complaint in the Introduction chapter again. Let us see what happens when the management and the advisor of this particular business get it right.

If you recall, Dot receives her new insurance policy in the post and has noticed some errors. Derek wants to get out of the house and meet with his friends for a while.

We pick this up at the point of the call starting.

Dot has got herself very 'worked up' and frustrated at the errors she has found. She has dialled the number given in the letter.

As the number was connecting and ringing, she practised what she was going to say under her breath, repeating over and over her first line. The call was answered and Dot readied herself to deliver the well-rehearsed opening.

She did not quite hear the first part of the recorded message, as it took a second or two to register that it was not a human voice, but as the recording said...

'Please choose from one of the following options,' she focussed on it and chose Customer Service.

'Good morning, APPLEX Insurance, Jane speaking. How can I help?' said Jane in a cheerful voice.

'Good morning,' replied Dot. **'I need to speak to someone about an error.'**

'Oh, sorry to hear that. I can look into this for you. Again, my name is Jane, can I have yours, please?'

Dot was quite pleased with the cheery nature, so much so she gave her first name, 'Yes, it is Dorothy, Dorothy Clarke. That is the problem, you have spelt Clarke wrong.'

'Oh dear,' said Jane, 'I am sure we can sort that out. I will need to ask you a couple of security questions and also to find your file, is that OK?'

'Go ahead,' said Dorothy, ready for the questioning.

'Can I have your postcode please?' said Jane.

'DH25 6TD,' said Dot.

'Can I have the first line of your address, please?' enquired Jane.

'Ivy Cottage, Wilderness Lane,' said Dot.

'That's fine, Mrs Clarke, I have all the details now,' said Jane reassuringly. She continued, 'OK, we have spelt your name incorrectly. Is there anything else I need to look into while I sort out that problem?'

Dot was impressed that she seemed to have got through straight away and had got a person who had taken ownership of the problem. 'Yes,' said Dot. 'There is another point, you have taken a premium for Garden Cover, but it is not on my policy.'

'Oh, sorry about that, Mrs Clarke. I really want to get these two points resolved as it must have been very annoying for you and certainly not a good first impression. I have to ask you to do something for me, is that OK?' said Jane without a pause.

Dot was now sitting back in her chair and Derek had put his paper down and was getting quite interested in Dot making a complaint call and NOT getting annoyed.

Jane continued, **'Can you please look on the page with the blue border in your pack and see if it says "GC Incl" there? It will be just under the picture of the boat.'**

Dot found that section immediately. **'Yes, it does say that.'**

'Brilliant,' said Jane. **'Garden Cover IS included, but that section is sent separately and you should get it by the weekend. I will give you a number to call if for any reason it does not arrive. I will also log that you had to call so when they review the paperwork, your call will be taken into account.'**

Dot was very pleased so far, so much so that she was waving to Derek for him to go out, mouthing in a loud whisper, **'Go off to the café, I will meet you down there.'**

Derek was out of the door before Dot returned to her call.

'Thank you, Jane, I do dislike all these forms. Now about my name, you have missed an "E" off of the end.'

'Oh, that's easily done. Have that changed in no time, but I am afraid I need to get somebody in the Admin Department to do that. I can call them and get the right person and then transfer you. Can I put you on hold for two minutes while I do that?'

'Certainly,' confirmed Dot. She sat up in her chair, leaned over to her tea and decided she had time to dunk a biscuit.

Just as the biscuit dropped into her tea with a plop, Jane was back.

'Thank you for holding. I was lucky, I spoke to someone there and then who has put your change on her work pile and will get a fresh pack of paperwork out to you. If this is not with you by Friday, you can call me again. I will put a note on your file on my computer so anyone else will see what has happened.'

'That is all fine,' said Dot. **'In fact, it is very good indeed... thank you.'**

Dot put her coat on and went to meet Derek, feeling very reassured about her new insurance company.

Lightning Source UK Ltd.
Milton Keynes UK
25 November 2010

163444UK00001B/313/P

9 781907 211850